W9-AUH-826

Potatoes!

Easy Ideas

AMERICAN ★COOKING★ GUILD™

Boynton Beach, Florida

Acknowledgments
—Recipes developed by the Current Test Kitchen
—Cover Design and Layout by Pearl & Associates, Inc.

Revised Edition 1997
Copyright © 1989, 1994 by Current, Inc.
All rights reserved.
Printed in U.S.A.
ISBN 0-942320-46-8

More...Quick Recipes for Creative Cooking!
The American Cooking Guild's *Collector's Series* includes over 30 popular cooking topics such as Barbeque, Breakfast & Brunches, Chicken, Cookies, Hors d' Oeuvres, Seafood, Tea, Coffee, Pasta, Pizza, Salads Italian and many more. Each book contains more than 50 selected recipes. For a catalog of these and many other full sized cookbooks, send $1 to the address below and a coupon will be included for $1 off your first order.

Cookbooks Make Great Premiums!
The American Cooking Guild has been the premier publisher of private label and custom cookbooks since 1981. Retailers, manufacturers, and food companies have all chosen The American Cooking Guild to publish their premium and promotional cookbooks. For further information on our special markets programs please contact the address.

The American Cooking Guild
3600-K South Congress Avenue
Boynton Beach, FL 33426

Contents

Potato Toppings

Potato Soups

Potato Salads

Main Dishes

Oven Side Dishes

Baked Goods

Introduction

What's a meal without potatoes? Mashed, baked, boiled or fried, the beloved potato reigns as the nation's most popular vegetable. Potatoes are a welcome addition to anyone's diet—they are low in fat and sodium, and high in fiber and complex carbohydrates. Despite their healthful goodness, potatoes are widely considered fattening food, when in fact it's what you put on them that accounts for most of the calories.

See the introductory pages of this book for some of the basic ways to cook potatoes without added ingredients. When you'd like to round out a meal with a hearty and satisfying potato accompaniment, move on to the chapters on soups, salads and side dishes. You'll find lots of tempting recipes such as Potato Chowder, Greek Luncheon Salad and Oven Potato Puff.

The main dish section features hearty potato entrées, with the addition of meat, fish, cheese, or eggs. Your family will enjoy flavorful Garden Stuffed Potatoes, Cheesy Potatoes and Chops, or German Potato Pancakes.

Baked goods, made the old-fashioned way with mashed or shredded potatoes, complete this extraordinary assortment of recipes. Nothing compares to the fresh-baked aroma of Jiffy Yeast Rolls, Old-Fashioned Chocolate Cake or Apricot Scones.

It's been a taste treat preparing this collection for you. We hope you will use it often to bring the homey goodness of potatoes to your family and friends.

About Potatoes

The humble, yet hearty potato has played an important part in the history and economy of Europe and the Americas. The potato we are familiar with today was discovered by the Spanish in Peru. They brought it back to Spain where it was eventually accepted. Later, its popularity spread to France, Russia, Germany and Ireland.

In the early 1800s, Irish immigrants brought their treasured family recipes to the United States and planted potatoes in large quantities where they settled. It wasn't long before meat, potatoes and gravy became the favorite all-American dinner.

The potato provides good nutrition and contains a modest number of calories. It is inexpensive and available year round. Its versatility makes the potato a staple in our diet; yet by itself, it is not "fattening" as many people think. Known as a "comfort food," our mouth may begin to water at the thought of a bowl of creamy mashed potatoes with gravy, a tantalizing variety of "toppings" at a baked potato bar, or the aroma of freshly baked potato rolls! As a declared potato lover, read on for helpful tips and a variety of delicious recipes to maximize the not-so-everyday potato!

Buying Tips

• Choose potatoes that are firm, fairly clean and have a smooth skin without any sprouts or blemishes, but not washed. Potatoes that have been washed will spoil quicker.

• Potatoes of a uniform size and shape will cook in about the same amount of time and will be easier to peel.

• A greenish cast or tint indicates potatoes have been exposed to light during storage, which may cause a bitter taste and may be toxic to some people. Avoid purchasing. (If present, peel and remove all green color before using.)

• Don't buy potatoes with wrinkled skins, sprouted eyes, soft spots, dark spots or cut surfaces.

Storage Tips

• Store in a well-ventilated cool, dry, dark area such as a cool closet or dry basement (not under the kitchen sink!).

• At 45° to 50°, potatoes keep well for several weeks. At room temperature or in a warm garage, potatoes will remain at top quality for about 1 week.

• Don't store in the refrigerator as the potato starch will begin to change to sugar, and the potatoes will turn dark after cooking.

Preparation Tips

• Soak potatoes briefly to loosen dirt and make scrubbing easier.

• Scrub gently with a vegetable brush or sponge and trim as needed.

• Leave the skin on the potatoes during cooking to conserve the nutrients.

• If peeling potatoes before cooking, keep peelings thin to avoid losing nutrients just under the skin.

• To prevent peeled potatoes from turning dark, cook immediately or cover with water and add a small amount of ascorbic acid, lemon juice, salt or even vinegar. Soaking too long in water will cause some loss of nutrients. However, soaking in chilled water for about 1 hour is often recommended when preparing French fries to remove some of the starch and produce a crisper product.

• When making potato dishes ahead, use cooked, not raw, potatoes or the mixture may discolor. Or, cook the mixture until almost done, cool and refrigerate. Complete cooking just before serving.

• Potatoes and mixtures with potatoes do not freeze well due to their tendency to become mushy when thawed and reheated. Baked stuffed potatoes, mashed potato patties and partially cooked French fries can be frozen.

How To Cook Potatoes

Here are cooking methods and hints for all the basic ways of cooking potatoes:

Boiled Potatoes

Scrub potatoes and peel if desired. Place potatoes in a saucepan, adding boiling water as needed to cover and about ½ teaspoon salt per quart of water. Cover tightly. After the water returns to a boil, reduce heat and simmer until potatoes are fork-tender. Small or cut-up potatoes will take 15 to 20 minutes to cook; whole medium potatoes will take 30 to 40 minutes. Drain well. Return pan to low heat and shake pan until potatoes are dry. If the potatoes are cooked before peeling, they will peel more easily while still warm.

Tip: Do not overcook potatoes or they may become watery. Adding a piece of onion to the cooking water will add flavor.

Steamed Potatoes

Scrub potatoes and peel if desired. Use a steamer or place a wire rack on the bottom of a large saucepan and add enough water to just reach the bottom of the rack. Bring the water to a boil; then add potatoes, cover tightly and cook until fork-tender. If the lid doesn't fit tightly, you may need to add more boiling water during cooking. Cooking time will be approximately the same as for boiling.

Tip: Small, new potatoes are especially good when steamed. Gently scrub the potatoes, then peel a thin strip from around the center to prevent the skins from bursting while steaming. They will be done in about 15 minutes and shouldn't be overcooked.

Riced Potatoes

Prepare boiled or steamed potatoes, then drain and peel. Force potatoes through a potato ricer or food mill. Add melted butter or margarine to the potatoes after ricing. They are best when served immediately. Potatoes can be riced when preparing mashed potatoes (see Mashed Potatoes, page 9).

Mashed Potatoes

Prepare boiled or steamed potatoes; then drain and peel. Mash potatoes using a potato masher, electric mixer or ricer until no lumps remain. Gradually add warm milk, salt, pepper and bits of butter or margarine. Beat potatoes with an electric mixer, whisk or a wooden spoon until light and fluffy, adding more warm milk until the desired creaminess. (Overbeating can cause potatoes to become gummy and sticky because the starch begins to break down.)

Tip: For 1 pound of potatoes, you will need about 2 tablespoons butter and ¼ to ½ cup warm milk. If not serving immediately, spoon potatoes into a buttered baking dish, dot with more butter, cover loosely and keep warm in a preheated 250° oven.

Baked Potatoes

You can bake potatoes in an oven or toaster oven, along with the rest of your dinner, by adjusting the time and temperature. A medium-sized potato will bake in 40 to 45 minutes at 425° but will take about 1¼ hours at 350°. Scrub, then prick the potato several times with a fork before baking to allow steam to escape and to prevent the skin from bursting. For a softer skin, rub with vegetable oil before baking. For a crustier skin, bake longer or in a hotter oven. Wrapping the potato in foil before or after baking gives a softer skin and helps to retain heat, but also causes steaming and a less mealy potato. For ease in handling hot potatoes, bake on a baking sheet or stand upright in muffin tins, allowing ample heat circulation between the potatoes. To test for doneness, pinch potatoes with a hot pad and fingers or pierce with a fork. With a knife, cut a slit or a cross on the top of the potato to release steam and assure a mealy texture.

Tip: Inserting an aluminum or stainless steel baking nail into a potato speeds up the baking time since it helps get the heat into the center. When you want baked potatoes in a hurry, cut them in half, coat cut edges with oil and place cut-side down on a baking sheet. Half of a medium-sized potato will be fork-tender in about 30 minutes. For a crowd, keep in mind that 20 potatoes will bake in about the same time as a single potato.

Pan Roasted Potatoes

Prepare boiled or steamed peeled potatoes, cooking only 10 minutes until barely tender; then drain and peel. Arrange in a shallow baking dish, brushing generously with melted butter or margarine. Bake uncovered in a preheated 400° oven for 40 to 45 minutes or until browned and fork-tender, turning occasionally and basting with more butter. When roasting with meat, arrange peeled, uncooked potatoes around the meat in a roasting pan during the last 1 to 1 ½ hours of cooking time. Turn potatoes frequently and baste with pan drippings until browned and fork-tender. Sprinkle with parsley, paprika or herbs before serving.

Boiled Potatoes In The Microwave

Scrub, then peel and quarter similar-sized potatoes. Place in a shallow baking dish and add about ¼ cup water; cover. Four medium (6 oz. each) potatoes will take 8 to 10 minutes at 100% power (HIGH) in a 700-watt microwave oven, stirring every 4 minutes to rearrange pieces and move potatoes in center to outside edge of dish. Cover and let stand for 3 minutes or until desired doneness.

Baked Potatoes In The Microwave

Select whole, slender, similar-sized potatoes. Scrub, then pierce each with a fork 10 to 12 times. Arrange in spoke fashion with smaller ends to the center and at least 1 inch apart on a double-thickness of paper towels in the microwave oven. Four medium (6 oz. each) potatoes will take 10 to 12 minutes at 100% power (HIGH) in a 700-watt microwave oven; rearrange and turn over once while cooking. Cover and let stand for 5 to 10 minutes or until uniformly soft when pinched with fingers.

Tip: For a single potato, microwave for about 4 minutes, turning over once. For each additional potato, add about 2 minutes.

French Fries

Peel raw potatoes and cut with a knife or crinkle cutter into ¼-inch slices, then strips about ¼ inch thick. Immediately place strips in a bowl of ice water to maintain crispness and prevent discoloration. You can soak the strips up to 1 hour to remove some of the starch; however, some of the nutrients will be lost. Pat strips very dry with paper towels. Meanwhile, heat about 4 to 5 inches of vegetable oil to 375° in a deep-fat fryer or large heavy saucepan. Place a handful of potato strips in a wire basket and immerse in the hot fat. (It is best to cook them in small batches.) Shake basket to prevent potatoes from sticking together. Cook about 5 minutes or until golden brown and tender. Drain well on several thicknesses of paper towels. Continue until all strips are cooked. Keep warm in a shallow pan in a preheated 300° oven. To prevent sogginess, salt lightly just before serving.

Tip: Potato strips can be fried directly in hot oil without a wire basket; when done, remove carefully with a slotted spoon.

Home Fries or Hash Browns

Prepare boiled or steamed potatoes; drain and peel if desired. Slice or dice ¼- to ⅜-inch thick. Stir in optional ingredients such as chopped onion or cooked ham; sprinkle with salt and pepper. Preheat a large skillet (preferably one with a non-stick finish) to 375° (medium high). Generously grease skillet with several tablespoons of shortening, vegetable oil, margarine, strained bacon fat or a combination. Place potatoes in skillet, tossing gently to coat all pieces. For best results, mixture should not be more than ¾-inch deep in skillet. Do not flatten potatoes with a spatula. Lightly toss mixture frequently during cooking until potatoes are tender and golden brown, 10 to 15 minutes. Add additional fat as needed to prevent sticking. Season with additional salt and pepper.

Grilled Potatoes

Tear off two 6 x 9-inch pieces of heavy-duty foil for each potato. Coat potato with vegetable oil or soft margarine. Place each potato in center of double thickness of foil. Season with salt and pepper. Bring two sides of foil together over food; fold edges several times to seal, allowing space for steam. Fold up short edges and pinch together to seal. Place on grill about 4 inches above medium-hot coals. Cook for 45 to 60 minutes or until tender, turning several times. (Adjust cooking time according to heat of coals and size of potatoes.)

Selecting The Best Potato

KIND OF POTATO	CHARACTERISTICS	BEST USES
Russet	slender, oval shape; rough brown skin with lots of eyes; mealy texture when cooked due to low moisture and high starch content; easily absorbs dressing, sauce or butter.	baking mashing frying
Red, White, Purple	round; keeps shape when cooked; waxy texture when cooked due to higher moisture and lower starch content; slow to absorb dressing, sauce or butter.	boiling salads scalloped creamed
New	small; not put into storage; tender skins; waxy texture when cooked; often in limited supply	boiling steaming salads

Nutrition Facts

One medium-sized uncooked potato (about 6 oz.) gives you:

- about 110 calories (It's the toppings that add the calories!)
- 50% Vitamin C (U.S. Recommended Daily Allowances)
- 15% B_6 (U.S. RDA)—which is hard to get in foods
- 15% Iodine (U.S. RDA)
- 10% Niacin (U.S. RDA)
- 8% Thiamin (U.S. RDA)
- 8% Iron (U.S. RDA)
- a good source of fiber (especially the peel)
- a good source of protein for a vegetable
- a good "storehouse" of minerals (potassium, magnesium, folacin or folic acid, copper and zinc)

POTATO
TOPPINGS

Basic Gravy For Potatoes

Pan drippings are the natural drippings (fat and juices) left in the skillet, broiler or roasting pan after cooking meat. Any brown particles left in the pan will give a richer brown color.

¼	cup pan drippings, butter or margarine
3 to 4	tablespoons all-purpose flour
2	cups water, milk or meat broth or a combination
	bottled browning and seasoning sauce, to taste
	salt, to taste
	pepper, to taste

In a small saucepan or skillet over medium heat, warm drippings. When hot, add flour. Cook and stir constantly until browned. Gradually stir in liquid. Stirring, bring to a boil and boil until smooth and thickened. If desired, add bottled browning and seasoning sauce for a richer color. Season with salt and pepper to taste.

Yield: about 2 cups

Potato Yields
About 3 medium potatoes equals 1 pound, which in turn yields:

- 3 cups peeled and sliced
- 2 cups French fries
- 2½ cups peeled and diced
- 2 cups mashed
- 2½ cups shredded
- 2 cups potato salad

Deluxe Blue Cheese Topping

Use as a topping for baked potatoes.

- ½ cup mayonnaise
- ½ cup dairy sour cream
- 1 tablespoon white vinegar
- 1 tablespoon grated onion
- ½ teaspoon sugar
- ⅛ teaspoon salt
- ⅛ teaspoon dry mustard
- ⅛ teaspoon garlic powder
  hot pepper sauce, to taste
- 2 ounces blue cheese, crumbled (about ¼ cup)

In a medium bowl, combine mayonnaise, sour cream, vinegar, onion, sugar, salt, mustard, garlic powder and hot pepper sauce. Stir in blue cheese. Cover and refrigerate several hours.

Yield: about 1 cup

Mock Sour Cream

This creamy topping makes a good low-cal base for dips and salad dressings.

- 1 cup low-fat (1%) cottage cheese
- ⅓ cup plain low-fat yogurt
- ¾ teaspoon lemon juice

Place cottage cheese, yogurt and lemon juice in a blender container. Cover and blend at medium speed until smooth and creamy, stopping to scrape sides occasionally. Transfer to a container. Cover and chill at least 1 hour. Stir before using.

Spoon on top of baked potatoes, adding chives and pepper.

Yield: about 1 cup

Herb Butter

Use as a topping for baked, mashed or Twice-Baked Potatoes. For the herbs, try dill, basil, marjoram or an Italian herb mixture.

- ½ cup butter or margarine, softened
- 1 tablespoon minced parsley
- 1½ teaspoons minced chives or green onion
- 1 teaspoon crushed dried herbs
- ¼ teaspoon salt, garlic salt or smoke-flavored salt
- ⅛ teaspoon pepper or dash of hot pepper sauce

In a small bowl, beat butter, parsley, chives, dried herbs, salt and pepper until well blended. Cover and chill at least 30 minutes.
Yield: about ½ cup

Zippy Cheddar Chili Topping

Use as a topping for baked potatoes. To make a dip, increase the sour cream to ¾ cup and eliminate the butter. Add salt to taste.

- 1 tablespoon water
- 2 teaspoons dried minced onion
- 1 cup shredded Cheddar cheese (4 oz.)
- ½ cup dairy sour cream
- ¼ cup butter or margarine, softened
- ½ of a 4-oz. can diced green chilies
  salt, to taste

In a small bowl, place water and onion. Let stand until softened. Stir in cheese, sour cream and butter until blended. Stir in green chilies and salt, to taste.
Yield: about 1⅓ cups

POTATO
SOUPS

Tavern Cheese Soup

The hearty flavor will remind you of wintery nights and fireside conversations.

5	cups peeled, diced russet potatoes (about 2 lbs.)
1½	cups water
1	cup chopped celery
1	cup chopped leeks
2	teaspoons chicken bouillon granules
8	ounces Cheddar cheese, shredded
2	cups milk
1	cup beer or water
2	teaspoons Worcestershire sauce
1	teaspoon salt
¼	teaspoon dry mustard
¼	teaspoon white pepper

In a large saucepan over high heat, bring potatoes, water, celery, leeks and bouillon granules to a boil. Reduce heat to low, cover and simmer for 30 minutes or until potatoes are fork-tender. Remove from heat (do not drain) and mash mixture until smooth.

Gently stir in cheese until melted. Stir in milk, beer, Worcestershire sauce, salt, dry mustard and white pepper. Stir over low heat until hot. Serve immediately.

Yield: about 6 one-cup servings

Potato-Vegetable Soup

For a main dish soup, add sliced knockwurst and heat through or sprinkle servings with shredded Cheddar cheese.

2	cups water
2	cups peeled, cubed potatoes (about ¾ lb.)
1	cup chopped green cabbage
½	cup sliced carrot
½	cup sliced celery
½	cup chopped onion
¼	cup milk or water
2	teaspoons chicken bouillon granules
⅛	teaspoon ground nutmeg
⅛	teaspoon pepper
	croutons or garlic bread, for serving

Place water, potatoes, cabbage, carrot, celery, onion, milk, bouillon granules, nutmeg and pepper in a large saucepan. Over medium-high heat, bring to a boil; reduce heat to low, cover and simmer for 25 to 30 minutes or until vegetables are tender.

To thicken the soup, place a cup of the mixture in a blender container or food processor bowl. Cover and blend or process until smooth. Return mixture to saucepan and heat through.

Garnish individual servings with nutmeg. Serve with croutons or garlic bread.

Yield: 4 one-cup servings

If a soup or stew tastes too salty, add a few slices of raw potato to the dish—the potato will absorb some of the excess salt. (Be sure to discard the potato before serving.)

Vichyssoise

This is a tasty appetizer for guests. Served hot in the winter or cold in the summer, it is delicious year round!

1	cup chopped celery with leaves
3	leeks, white part only, sliced ¼ inch thick
½	cup chopped onion
2	tablespoons butter or margarine
1	cup dry vermouth
1	cup water
3	medium russet potatoes, peeled, cut in cubes (3 cups)
¼	cup chopped parsley
3	teaspoons chicken bouillon granules
¼	teaspoon salt
2	cups half-and-half
¼	teaspoon white pepper
	butter, if desired
	chopped chives, as garnish

In a 3-quart saucepan over medium heat, sauté celery, leeks and onion in butter for 10 minutes, or until limp and golden. Stir in vermouth and water. Add potatoes, parsley, bouillon granules and salt. Bring to a boil; reduce heat to low, cover and simmer for 20 to 25 minutes or until vegetables are very tender. Stir in half-and-half and white pepper. Taste for additional seasoning.

To purée, place 2 cups of the mixture at a time in a blender container or food processor. Cover and blend or process until very smooth.

To serve hot, reheat over low heat, stirring often to prevent scorching. If desired, garnish individual servings with a pat of butter and sprinkle with chives.

To serve cold, refrigerate puréed mixture for several hours. Serve in chilled cups and garnish with chives.

Yield: about 6 one-cup servings

Rich Cream of Spinach Soup

This is sometimes called "Russian Vichyssoise." If you prefer, substitute two cups chopped fresh spinach for the frozen.

1	package (10 oz.) frozen leaf spinach, thawed
1	cup chopped onion
¼	cup butter or margarine
3	medium potatoes, peeled and quartered (about 1 lb.)
1	can (10¾ oz.) double-strength chicken broth
1½	cups water
2	teaspoons chicken bouillon granules
2	cups half-and-half
½	teaspoon salt
⅛	teaspoon pepper
¾	cup dairy sour cream
	additional dairy sour cream, for garnish
	ground allspice, optional

Squeeze spinach dry; coarsely chop and set aside.

In a large saucepan over medium heat, sauté onion in butter for 3 minutes or until limp. Add potatoes, chicken broth, water and bouillon granules. Bring to a boil; reduce heat to low, cover and simmer for 20 to 25 minutes or until potatoes are tender. Add spinach and cook for 2 to 4 minutes or until spinach is tender.

Place small batches of mixture at a time in a blender container. Cover and blend until puréed. Return mixture to saucepan. Whisk in half-and-half, salt and pepper.

Over low heat, bring to just under boiling. Whisk in sour cream.

Soup can be served hot or chilled. Stir before serving. To serve, garnish individual servings with additional sour cream or, if desired, sprinkle with allspice.

Yield: 6 to 8 servings

Potato Chowder

This chowder has a rich flavor. If you wish, add chopped clams for a seafood chowder.

½ pound lean bacon, cut in ½-inch pieces
½ cup finely chopped cooked ham
1 cup chopped onion
½ cup thinly sliced celery
2 tablespoons all-purpose flour
4 cups peeled, diced potatoes (about 1½ lbs.)
½ cup hot water
3 cups milk
¾ teaspoon salt
⅛ teaspoon pepper
2 cans (6½ oz. each) minced or chopped clams, optional
1 tablespoon dried parsley flakes
butter, as garnish
paprika, as garnish

In a deep 12-inch skillet or 3-quart saucepan over medium heat, fry bacon and ham until brown. Remove with a slotted spoon; set aside. Discard all but 2 tablespoons of the drippings.

To skillet, add onion and celery. Sauté until limp. Sprinkle with flour, stirring until blended. Stir in potatoes, hot water, bacon and ham. Reduce heat to low, cover and simmer for 20 to 25 minutes or until potatoes are very tender. Stir in milk, salt and pepper. If desired, add clams with liquid and parsley. Bring to a boil, cover and simmer for 5 minutes or until heated through.

Ladle into soup bowls. Top each serving with a pat of butter and a sprinkle of paprika.

Yield: about 6 one-cup servings

Vegetable Soup With Pesto

If you prefer, substitute frozen cut green beans for the fresh beans.

- 4 cups water
- 3 medium potatoes, finely chopped (about 1 Ib.)
- ¾ pound fresh green beans, cut in 1-inch pieces (about 3 cups)
- 2 medium tomatoes, quartered, seeded and chopped
- ½ teaspoon salt
  dash of pepper
- ¾ cup broken vermicelli
- 8 medium mushrooms, sliced
- 1 recipe Pesto Sauce, prepared
  grated Parmesan cheese, as garnish

In a 5-quart Dutch oven, place water, potatoes, green beans, tomatoes, salt and pepper. Over high heat, bring to a boil; reduce heat to medium-low, cover and simmer for 8 minutes. Add vermicelli and mushrooms. Return to a boil and cook 8 minutes longer or until vegetables and vermicelli are tender.

Prepare Pesto Sauce as directed. Stir ½ cup of Pesto into the soup and heat through. Ladle into bowls and garnish each serving with a little Pesto Sauce and a sprinkle of Parmesan cheese.

Yield: about 9 one-cup servings

Pesto Sauce

- ⅓ cup fresh basil leaves or 1½ tablespoons dried basil
- ¼ cup fresh parsley (tightly packed)
- 1 medium tomato, quartered and seeded
- 3 cloves garlic, crushed
- ¼ cup grated Parmesan cheese
- ¼ cup olive oil

Place first four ingredients in a blender. Cover and blend. Add Parmesan cheese; blend again. With motor running, slowly add olive oil until mixture is well blended. Makes about 1 cup.

POTATO
SALADS

Light Potato Salad

Lots of flavor without a heavy dressing.

4	cups cooked, peeled and diced red potatoes (1½ lbs.)
1	cup thinly sliced celery
¼	cup sliced green onions
¼	cup chopped red pepper
1	tablespoon chopped parsley
⅔	cup plain low-fat yogurt
¼	cup reduced-calorie mayonnaise or salad dressing
1	tablespoon Dijon mustard
1	teaspoon salt
8	drops hot pepper sauce
	paprika, as garnish
	parsley sprigs, as garnish

Place potatoes, celery, green onions, red pepper and parsley in a large bowl.

In a medium bowl, stir yogurt, salad dressing, Dijon mustard, salt and hot pepper sauce until blended. Pour over potato mixture and stir gently. Transfer to a serving bowl. Cover and refrigerate for 1 to 4 hours.

Sprinkle with paprika and garnish with parsley sprigs before serving.

Yield: 8 servings

Greek Luncheon Salad

Serve with bread and a dessert for a complete meal.

- ½ cup olive or vegetable oil
- ¼ cup lemon juice
- 1 clove garlic, minced
- ½ teaspoon dried oregano leaves, crushed
- ¼ teaspoon salt
- ¼ teaspoon dried rosemary leaves, crushed
- ⅛ teaspoon pepper
- 2 cups cubed cooked potatoes (about 2 medium)
- 1 can (7¾ oz.) red or (6½ oz.) pink salmon
  lettuce leaves
- 4 cups chopped iceberg lettuce
- 1 large cucumber, peeled, halved lengthwise and sliced
- 6 ounces feta cheese, crumbled
- 1 can (3¼ oz.) pitted ripe or Greek olives
- 2 medium tomatoes, chopped
- ⅓ cup sliced green onions
- 3 tablespoons capers, drained

In a small bowl, whisk oil, lemon juice, garlic, oregano, salt, rosemary and pepper until blended. Place potatoes in a shallow dish. Drizzle with 2 tablespoons of the dressing and toss lightly; set potatoes and remaining dressing aside.

Drain salmon, remove bones and dark skin. Break into bite-size chunks; set aside.

Line a large shallow bowl with lettuce leaves. Add chopped lettuce and cucumber. Arrange potatoes, feta cheese, salmon and olives in a decorative design on top. Place tomatoes around edge. Sprinkle with green onions and capers. Pour half of the dressing over salad. Pass remaining dressing separately.

Yield: 4 large servings

Deli Potato Salad

The horseradish blends nicely with the other ingredients. A favorite for potluck suppers. Serve in a colorful bowl.

8	cups russet potatoes, cooked, peeled and cubed (3 lb.)
½	cup beef broth or bouillon
⅔	cup dairy sour cream
⅓	cup mayonnaise
¼	cup sliced green onions
3	tablespoons prepared horseradish
1½	tablespoons prepared mustard
1	tablespoon lemon juice
½	teaspoon celery seeds
	salt and pepper, to taste
1	cup thinly sliced celery
4	hard-cooked eggs, chopped
3	tablespoons sliced pimiento

Place potatoes in a large bowl. Pour in broth and toss gently. Let stand for 30 minutes.

Meanwhile, in a medium bowl, mix sour cream, mayonnaise, green onions, horseradish, mustard, lemon juice, celery seeds, salt and pepper until well blended. Add to potatoes along with celery, eggs and pimiento. Gently toss until potatoes are well coated. Cover and refrigerate at least 2 hours.

Let stand at room temperature about 30 minutes before serving.

Yield: 8 to 12 servings

Garden Fresh Salad

If you haven't used jicama before, you will be pleasantly surprised by this sweet, crunchy vegetable. If you don't have jicama, substitute a can of well-drained sliced water chestnuts.

3	medium potatoes (about 1 lb.)
½	teaspoon salt
⅛	teaspoon pepper
1½	cups broccoli florets, cut in bite-size pieces
1	cup jicama, peeled and cut in 1-inch long julienne strips
½	cup chopped green pepper
¼	cup chopped fresh parsley or basil leaves
⅓	cup Italian or vinaigrette salad dressing
	red-tipped leaf lettuce, to line serving bowl
¼	cup shredded carrot
2	tablespoons sliced green onions

Cook potatoes in boiling salted water until tender. Drain well. When cool enough to handle, peel and dice. Place in a medium bowl. Sprinkle with salt and pepper; toss lightly. Cool to room temperature.

Meanwhile, steam broccoli until crisp-tender. Drain and cool. Add broccoli, jicama, green pepper and parsley to potatoes. Pour dressing over, tossing until coated. Chill for 30 minutes.

To serve, spoon into a lettuce-lined bowl. Garnish with carrot and sliced green onions.

Yield: 4 to 6 servings

Hot German Potato Salad

This traditional German dish makes a delicious accompaniment to bratwurst.

2	pounds boiling potatoes (about 6)
6	slices bacon
1	cup sliced celery
¾	cup chopped onion
1	tablespoon all-purpose flour
1	tablespoon sugar
1	teaspoon salt
⅛	teaspoon pepper
¾	cup water
2	tablespoons cider vinegar
1	tablespoon spicy brown mustard

Cook potatoes in boiling salted water until tender. Drain and cool. Peel if desired. Slice ¼-inch thick.

In a large skillet over medium heat, fry bacon until crisp. Remove with a slotted spoon; drain on paper towels. Discard all but 3 tablespoons of the drippings.

Over medium heat, sauté celery and onion in bacon drippings until lightly browned and crisp-tender. Stir in flour, sugar, salt and pepper until blended. Stir in water, vinegar and spicy brown mustard. Stirring constantly over medium heat, bring to a boil and boil until thickened. Remove from heat.

Crumble four slices of the bacon. Stir crumbled bacon and potatoes into hot dressing in skillet. Stirring gently, cook over medium heat until heated through and potatoes are well coated. Transfer to a serving bowl. Crumble remaining two slices of bacon and sprinkle over the top. Serve warm.

Yield: 6 servings

MAIN DISHES

Pizza Stuffed Spuds

The pizza flavors makes this popular with kids.

    4   medium baking potatoes
    ⅔   cup milk
    ¼   cup grated Parmesan cheese
    ¾   cup shredded mozzarella cheese (about 3 oz.)
    3   ounces pepperoni or salami, chopped (about ½ cup)
    1   teaspoon dried parsley flakes
    ½   cup pizza or spaghetti sauce

Bake potatoes (see page 9).

Slice off the top of each potato. Discard. Carefully spoon out centers, leaving about ½-inch shell.

Place potato pulp in a medium bowl and mash until smooth. Stir in milk and Parmesan cheese until blended. Stir in ½ cup of the mozzarella cheese, pepperoni and parsley. Mound potato mixture into shells. Arrange shells on a baking sheet. Spoon 2 tablespoons sauce over each.

Sprinkle with remaining mozzarella cheese. Bake in a 400° oven for 5 to 8 minutes or until hot and cheese melts.

Yield: 4 servings

Savory Puff Pastries

An elegant, easy-to-make entrée for a luncheon or light supper.

1 package (17¼ oz.) frozen puff pastry sheets
6 ounces sliced smoked cooked ham
1 cup diced cooked potato
2 tablespoons thinly sliced green onions
dash of pepper
1 jar (2¼ oz.) sliced pimento, drained
1 egg, slightly beaten
2½ tablespoons all-purpose flour
¼ cup butter or margarine
1¾ cups half-and-half
2 tablespoons Madeira or dry sherry
1½ teaspoons Dijon mustard
¾ teaspoon chicken bouillon granules
⅛ teaspoon pepper
parsley sprigs, as garnish

Partially thaw puff pastry sheets according to package directions, about 20 minutes.

Dice cooked ham (you will need about 1 cup). In a medium bowl, gently toss ham, potato, green onions and pepper; set aside.

Unfold pastry sheets, pressing together any torn areas. Cut each sheet into six rectangles (about 5 x 3 ¼ inches each). Dip a small (1 to 2-inch) decorative cookie cutter into flour; then cut a design in center of six of the rectangles, but do not remove the cut pastry. These cuts will rise up to form a "top hat" when baked.

In the center of each remaining six rectangles, spread about ⅓ cup of the ham-potato filling, leaving a ½-inch border. If desired, reserve twelve long pimiento slices for garnish; sprinkle remaining pimiento on top of ham filling. Brush borders with beaten egg. Place decorative rectangles over each filled portion. Press edges together and seat with the tines of a fork.*

Brush tops with remaining egg. Transfer to an ungreased baking sheet.

Place in the center of a preheated 400° oven. Immediately reduce oven temperature to 350° and bake for 40 to 45 minutes or until crisp and golden brown.

Meanwhile, in a small saucepan over medium heat, stir flour into melted butter. Cook and stir for 1 minute. Stir in half-and-half, Madeira, Dijon mustard, bouillon granules and pepper until smooth. Cook, stirring frequently, until mixture comes to a boil and is thickened. Remove from heat. Cover and keep warm. Stir before serving.

To serve, spoon about ⅓ cup of the sauce into the center of each serving plate. Place a pastry on top of sauce. Garnish with parsley and reserved pimento. Pass remaining sauce.

*Individual servings can be made to this point, then covered and refrigerated up to 4 hours. Transfer to a room-temperature baking sheet; brush with egg. Bake as directed.

If sauce is prepared ahead, place a piece of plastic wrap directly on the surface and refrigerate. Remove plastic wrap and reheat sauce over low heat, stirring frequently, about 10 minutes.

Yield: 6 servings

Deep-Dish Cottage Pie

This is a great way to use up leftover mashed potatoes. If you prefer, substitute cubed cooked turkey for the ground beef.

1	large onion, coarsely chopped
1	clove garlic, minced
2	tablespoons butter or margarine
1½	pounds extra-lean ground beef
3	large carrots, peeled and shredded
⅔	cup beef broth or bouillon
1	tablespoon tomato paste
1	teaspoon minced parsley
½	teaspoon dried thyme leaves, crushed
½	teaspoon dried sage leaves, crushed
1	teaspoon salt
⅛	teaspoon pepper
5	medium potatoes (about 1½ lbs.)
¾	cup warm milk
½	cup shredded Cheddar cheese (about 2 oz.)
½	cup grated Parmesan cheese

Grease an 8 x 8 x 2-inch baking dish.

In a large skillet over medium-high heat, sauté onion and garlic in butter until tender. Add beef and brown, breaking up meat. Stir in carrots, broth, tomato paste, parsley, thyme, sage, salt and pepper. Reduce heat to low and simmer for 30 minutes. Spoon mixture into baking dish.

Meanwhile, peel and cook potatoes. Mash, adding milk. (You will need about 3 cups mashed potatoes.) Spread mashed potatoes over top of meat mixture. In a small bowl, combine cheeses and sprinkle over potatoes.

Bake in a preheated 375° oven for 10 to 15 minutes or until cheese melts and top is golden brown.

Yield: 6 to 8 servings

Potatoes Jubilee

A 4-ounce jar of drained sliced pimientos can be used in place of the red pepper; add with the corn.

4	medium baking potatoes
6	slices bacon, cut in pieces
½	cup chopped red pepper
¼	cup chopped green pepper
¼	cup sliced green onions
1	cup corn, fresh or thawed if frozen
1	cup evaporated milk
1	tablespoon dried parsley flakes
¼	teaspoon salt
⅛	teaspoon pepper
6	ounces Monterey Jack cheese, shredded (1½ cups)
4	tablespoons butter or margarine

Bake potatoes (see page 9).

Meanwhile, in a large skillet over medium heat, fry bacon until crisp. Remove bacon with a slotted spoon, drain on paper towels; set aside for garnish. Discard all but 1 tablespoon of the drippings.

Sauté red pepper, green pepper and green onions in drippings until tender, but not browned. Add corn, evaporated milk, parsley, salt and pepper. Bring to a boil, reduce heat to low and simmer for 5 minutes or until slightly thickened. Stir in cheese until melted. Remove from heat; keep warm if necessary.

To serve, place each potato on a plate. Split potato in half lengthwise (do not separate) and fluff insides with a fork. For each potato, mix in 1 tablespoon butter; top with one-fourth of the corn mixture and garnish with reserved bacon.

Yield: 4 servings

Garden Stuffed Potatoes

An easy make-ahead dish.

4	medium baking potatoes (about 1½ lbs.)
2	packages (10 oz. each) frozen broccoli, carrots and cauliflower in cheese sauce, cooked as directed
1¼	cups diced cooked ham or turkey, optional
½	cup grated Parmesan cheese
¼	cup butter or margarine
6 to 8	drops hot pepper sauce

Bake potatoes (see page 9).

Slice off the top of each potato. Discard top. Carefully spoon out center pulp, leaving about a ½-inch shell.

Place pulp in a medium bowl and mash until smooth. Stir in vegetables with sauce, ham, Parmesan, butter and hot pepper sauce. Spoon into potato shells. Wrap individually in foil and bake, or refrigerate up to 24 hours.

Bake the foil-wrapped potatoes in a preheated 350° oven for 30 minutes. Open foil and broil 6 inches from heat source for 3 to 4 minutes, or until golden brown.

Yield: 4 servings

If you prefer baked potatoes with softer skins, rub each potato with a little vegetable oil before baking.

Mexican Stuffed Potatoes

This makes a filling vegetarian entrée for those of us trying to cut back on eating so much meat.

4   medium baking potatoes (about 1½ lbs.)
2   tablespoons diced onion
1   teaspoon butter or margarine
2   teaspoons all-purpose flour
1   medium zucchini, halved lengthwise, sliced ¼-inch thick
½   cup hot water
2   tablespoons chopped green pepper
1   teaspoon beef bouillon granules
1   medium tomato, cut in chunks
2   tablespoons diced green chilies
½   teaspoon chili powder
1   cup shredded sharp Cheddar cheese

Bake potatoes (see page 9).

Meanwhile, in a large non-stick skillet over medium heat, sauté onion in butter for 3 minutes or until transparent. Sprinkle with flour, stirring to coat. Stir in zucchini, water, green pepper and bouillon granules. Bring to a boil; reduce heat to low, cover and simmer for 3 minutes. Add tomato, green chiles and chili powder. Cover and simmer 1 to 2 minutes longer or until vegetables are crisp-tender.

Cut a cross on the top of each potato and fluff the insides with a fork. Place in individual ramekins or in an 8 x 8 x 2-inch baking pan.

Sprinkle each potato with 2 tablespoons of the cheese, spoon on one-fourth of the vegetable mixture and top with 2 tablespoons additional cheese.

Bake potatoes in a 400° oven for 3 minutes or until cheese melts. If desired, serve with cherry peppers and garnish with parsley sprigs.

Yield: 4 servings

Country Brunch Potatoes

If making ahead, top with crushed potato chips just before baking and increase baking time slightly.

4	medium boiling potatoes, cooked (about 1¼ lbs.)
3	hard-cooked eggs
¼	pound mushrooms, sliced (about 2 cups)
¼	cup sliced green onions, including some green
2	tablespoons butter or margarine
3	tablespoons all-purpose flour
¾	cup dairy sour cream
½	cup milk
¼	teaspoon paprika
	salt and pepper, to taste
5	slices processed American cheese (about 4 oz. total)
1	cup crushed sour cream-and-onion flavored potato chips

Preheat oven to 350°. Grease a shallow 1½-quart baking dish.

Peel and slice potatoes (you will need about 4 cups). Cut each egg into six wedges; set potatoes and eggs aside.

In a small saucepan over medium heat, sauté mushrooms and green onions in butter until limp. Add flour. Cook and stir for 1 minute. Stir in sour cream, milk, paprika, salt and pepper. Reduce heat to low. Break cheese into pieces; add to mixture. Cook and stir until cheese melts.

Place half of the potatoes in baking dish. Layer in order, half of the sauce, all of the egg wedges, remaining potatoes and remaining sauce, spreading sauce to coat top of potatoes. Sprinkle with potato chips.

Bake for 25 to 30 minutes or until bubbly and very hot.

Yield: 6 one-cup servings

Cheesy Potatoes and Chops

A favorite combination with lots of down-home flavor.

4	tenderloin pork chops
1½	teaspoons dried Italian herb seasoning, crushed
½	teaspoon garlic powder
¼	teaspoon salt
⅛	teaspoon pepper
2	tablespoons vegetable oil
1	can (11 oz.) condensed Cheddar cheese soup
1	can (10 ¾ oz.) condensed cream of mushroom soup
½	cup water
4	medium potatoes (about 1¼ lbs.)
1	medium onion, thinly sliced
	chopped parsley, as garnish

Preheat oven to 350°.

Trim excess fat from chops. In a small bowl, mix Italian seasoning, garlic powder, salt and pepper. Sprinkle half of the herb mixture onto chops and rub in.

In a large skillet over medium-high heat, brown both sides of chops in hot oil. Arrange in a single layer in a shallow 2-quart baking dish; set aside.

Reduce heat to low. Pour off excess drippings from skillet. Add soups and water, stirring to loosen browned bits on bottom of skillet; set aside.

Meanwhile, peel potatoes. Slice into a large bowl (you should have about 4 cups). Add onion and remaining herb mixture, tossing to coat well. Spread on top of chops. Evenly pour soup mixture over potatoes. Cover tightly with foil.

Bake for 1½ hours or until chops and potatoes are tender.

Garnish with parsley before serving.

Yield: 4 servings

Favorite Brunch Omelets

Rich and hearty, this dish makes a light supper with a green salad and bread.

2	slices bacon, cut in ½-inch pieces
1	cup diced cooked potato
2	tablespoons sliced green onions
1	clove garlic, minced
4	eggs
1	tablespoon water
¼	teaspoon salt
	dash of pepper
1	tablespoon butter or margarine
½	cup shredded Fontina or Monterey Jack cheese

In a medium saucepan over medium heat, sauté bacon until crisp. Add potato, green onions and garlic. Cook and stir until heated through; set aside and keep warm.

Meanwhile, in a medium bowl, whisk eggs, water, salt and pepper just until blended.

In a 7-inch non-stick skillet over medium-high heat, melt half of the butter until it foams. Rotate skillet to coat sides. When foam subsides, pour half of the egg mixture into skillet. Stir in a circular motion for 30 seconds. As outer edges set, use an inverted pancake turner to lift edges and tilt skillet so uncooked egg can flow to bottom. When center is creamy and edges are set to desired doneness, spoon half of the potato mixture over one side of omelet. Run a spatula around edge of omelet. Fold unfilled side over filled side.

Tilt skillet and slide onto a warmed plate. Sprinkle with half of the cheese. Cover with a lid to keep warm and melt the cheese. Repeat with remaining butter, egg mixture, potato filling and cheese. Serve immediately.

Yield: 2 servings

German Potato Pancakes

Shred the potatoes just before mixing and cooking to keep them from darkening. These pancakes are delicious served with applesauce.

1	egg
2	tablespoons all-purpose flour
2	cups peeled, shredded russet potatoes (about 1 lb.)
2	tablespoons grated onion
½	teaspoon salt
¼	teaspoon pepper
2	tablespoons butter or margarine
2	tablespoons vegetable oil
	hot applesauce, as an accompaniment

In a medium bowl, beat egg lightly; stir in flour until blended.

Using dry paper towels, squeeze all excess moisture from the shredded potatoes.

Stir potatoes, onion, salt and pepper into the egg mixture.

In a 10-inch skillet over medium-high heat, melt butter with oil. For each pancake, spoon 2 tablespoons of the potato mixture into skillet. Flatten each with a spatula into a 3-inch round. Fry each side for 2 to 3 minutes or until crisp and golden brown. Place fried pancakes in a single layer on a baking sheet and keep warm in a preheated 200° oven while frying the remaining pancakes.

Serve immediately with applesauce.

Yield: 12 (3-inch) pancakes

Tuna-Tater Casserole

Cooked chicken or turkey can be used in place of the tuna. You can use cream of chicken soup instead of cream of mushroom, if you prefer.

2   medium potatoes (about ¾ lb.)
1   can (6½ oz.) tuna, drained and flaked
1   package (10 oz.) frozen mixed vegetables
8   ounces Cheddar cheese, shredded (about 2 cups)
1   can (10¾ oz.) condensed cream of mushroom soup
½   cup milk
2   tablespoons minced onion
    paprika

Preheat oven to 350°. Generously butter a deep 2-quart baking dish.

Peel and dice potatoes. Place half of the potatoes in baking dish. Layer with tuna, then frozen vegetables and cheese. Top with remaining potatoes.

In a small bowl, stir soup, milk and onion until blended. Pour over potatoes.

Bake, uncovered, for 1 hour or until potatoes are tender and sauce is bubbly around edges. Sprinkle with paprika.

Yield: 4 to 6 servings

Italian Potato Pie

This hearty meal-in-one dish is ready in about 45 minutes.

1	pound mild bulk Italian sausage*
¾	cup coarsely chopped green pepper
¾	cup chopped onion
2	cloves garlic, minced
1	tablespoon olive oil
2	medium tomatoes, diced
8	medium mushrooms, sliced
1	can (2¼ oz.) sliced ripe olives, drained
1	teaspoon dried basil leaves, crushed
¼	teaspoon salt
⅛	teaspoon pepper
2½	cups seasoned mashed potatoes
¼	cup grated Parmesan cheese
2	tablespoons chopped fresh parsley or basil leaves

Preheat oven to 350°.

Crumble sausage into a cold skillet. Over medium heat, stir until browned; drain off fat. Spoon meat into a 9 x 9 x 2-inch or shallow 1½-quart baking dish; set aside.

In skillet over medium heat, sauté green pepper, onion and garlic in hot olive oil for 5 minutes or until onion is crisp-tender. Stir in tomatoes, mushrooms, olives, basil, salt and pepper; remove from heat.

Meanwhile, spread mashed potatoes over meat, spreading to edges of dish and smoothing surface. Spoon sautéed vegetables over potatoes to within 1 inch of edge of dish. Sprinkle top with Parmesan cheese and parsley.

Bake for 30 to 35 minutes or until very hot and top is lightly browned.

*If you prefer, substitute browned ground beef, seasoned with ½ teaspoon salt and ¼ teaspoon pepper, for the sausage.

Yield: 4 hearty servings

OVEN
SIDE DISHES

Razorback Potatoes

These oval-shaped potatoes make an attractive dish.

6   baking potatoes, 3 inches long
    salt and pepper, to taste
½   cup butter or margarine
½   cup grated Parmesan cheese
⅓   cup dry bread crumbs
    paprika, as garnish

Preheat oven to 450°. Generously grease a large shallow baking dish; set aside.

Peel potatoes to a uniform size. Starting at one end, cut ¼-inch slices without cutting all the way through to the bottom (slices will fan out slightly). Place potatoes in baking dish, cut-edge up. Sprinkle with salt and pepper, to taste. Dot with butter.

Bake for 20 minutes, basting occasionally with butter from bottom of dish.

Meanwhile, in a small bowl, mix Parmesan cheese and bread crumbs.

Remove the potatoes from oven. Sprinkle cheese-bread crumb mixture between potato slices and over top. Bake 25 to 30 minutes longer, without basting, or until golden brown and tender. Sprinkle with paprika.

Yield: 6 servings

Hacienda Potatoes

A unique combination of ingredients.

2	pounds small red potatoes
¼	cup diced green chilies, drained
3	tablespoons freshly grated Parmesan cheese
2	large cloves garlic, crushed
3	tablespoons olive oil
¼	cup sliced green onions
1½	teaspoons chicken bouillon granules
¾	teaspoon ground cumin
¼	teaspoon salt
¼	teaspoon hot pepper sauce
½	cup half-and-half
2	small firm tomatoes, sliced ¼-inch thick
	cilantro or parsley sprigs, as garnish
	additional sliced green onions, as garnish

In a large saucepan, cook potatoes in boiling salted water until tender. Drain, cool slightly and peel. Cut in half if large. Slice about ⅜-inch thick. (You will need about 5 cups.) Arrange slices around outer edge of a greased 1-quart shallow baking dish or 9-inch deep-dish pie plate, overlapping edges, then filling in the center of the dish. Sprinkle chilies and 2 tablespoons of the Parmesan cheese over potatoes.

Preheat oven to 400°. Meanwhile, in a small skillet over medium heat, sauté garlic in hot olive oil until lightly browned; discard garlic. Quickly stir in green onions, bouillon granules, cumin, salt and hot pepper sauce, then half-and-half. Bring to a boil, then spoon over potatoes. Arrange tomato slices in a pinwheel design in center of dish. Sprinkle tomatoes with remaining 1 tablespoon Parmesan cheese.

Bake for 25 minutes or until edges are bubbly and potatoes are lightly browned. Garnish with cilantro and green onions.

Yield: 6 servings

Oven Potato Puff

Just delicious for a buffet. Tastes like the stuffing in Twice-Baked Potatoes only lighter and fluffier.

          5   baking potatoes, peeled and quartered (about 2 lb.)
          1   cup small curd cottage cheese
          2   eggs
          1   cup dairy sour cream
          ⅓   cup chopped green onions
          ¼   cup butter or margarine, softened
          1   teaspoon salt
          ⅛   teaspoon pepper
          2   tablespoons butter or margarine, melted

In a 3-quart covered saucepan, cook potatoes in boiling salted water for 20 minutes or until very tender. Drain well and mash. (You will need about 6 cups.) Cover and set aside.

Butter a 2-quart round baking dish. In a large mixer bowl at high speed, beat cottage cheese and eggs for 2 minutes or until almost smooth. At low speed, beat in sour cream, green onions, softened butter, salt and pepper, scraping bowl as needed.

Add potatoes and beat until well blended. Transfer mixture to baking dish. If making ahead, cover and refrigerate until 30 minutes before baking.

Drizzle top of potatoes with melted butter. Bake in a preheated 325° oven for 50 to 60 minutes or until heated in center and top is lightly browned.

Yield: 8 servings

Twice-Baked Potatoes

Try one of the variations for a hearty lunch.

4	medium baking potatoes (about 1½ lbs.)
2	tablespoons butter or margarine, softened
½	teaspoon salt
	dash of pepper
½	cup warm milk, or more to taste
	paprika or additional butter, as garnish

Bake potatoes (see page 9).

Slice off the top ¼ inch of each potato. Discard top. Carefully spoon out center pulp, leaving about ½-inch shell.

Place pulp in a medium bowl and mash until smooth. Stir in butter, salt and pepper and enough milk to moisten. Beat until light and fluffy.

Mound into shells. Place on an ungreased baking sheet. Sprinkle with paprika or dot with additional butter if desired.

Bake in a preheated 375° oven for 15 to 20 minutes or until heated through.

Yield: 4 servings

Cheese-Bacon Stuffed Potatoes: Mash potatoes as directed. Stir in ½ cup shredded sharp Cheddar or Swiss cheese, 3 tablespoons crumbled cooked bacon and 1 tablespoon each minced onion and parsley before mounding into shells.

Ranch-Style Stuffed Potatoes: Mash potatoes as directed. Beat in ¾ cup low-fat cottage cheese or 3 oz. softened cream cheese, 1 tablespoon minced green onion and ½ teaspoon lemon juice. Fill shells and bake. Garnish with chopped tomatoes and diced onion.

Herb Stuffed Potatoes: Stir in 1 tablespoon fresh snipped chives or a mixture of ¾ teaspoon dried crushed herbs such as parsley, basil and thyme or dill. Taste and adjust seasoning before filling potato shells. Bake. Garnish with sautéed mushrooms, paprika and parsley sprigs.

Festive Potatoes Dauphine

Great for entertaining. Delicious served with pork chops or baked chicken breasts.

1¾	pounds baking potatoes, peeled
⅓	cup grated onion
2	tablespoons butter or margarine, melted
2	large eggs, lightly beaten
½	cup warm milk
⅔	cup ground almonds
½	cup shredded Cheddar or Colby cheese
½	teaspoon salt
⅛	teaspoon ground nutmeg
	dash of pepper
¼	cup sliced almonds, as garnish
2	tablespoons butter or margarine

In a 3-quart saucepan, cook potatoes in boiling salted water until very tender. Drain well.

Preheat oven to 400°. Butter a shallow 1½-quart baking dish.

Mash potatoes until no lumps remain. Stir in onion, then melted butter and eggs. Gradually add milk to mixture, beating until fluffy. Stir in ground almonds, cheese, salt, nutmeg and pepper until blended. Spoon into baking dish. Sprinkle sliced almonds over the top. Dot with pieces of butter.

Bake for 22 to 25 minutes or until very hot and top is golden brown.

Yield: 6 to 8 servings

Potato Kisses

Restaurants sometimes serve these with a steak or lamb chops. They are easily made at home.

2 cups stiff, smooth mashed potatoes
¼ cup dairy sour cream, or more as needed
¼ cup butter or margarine, melted and cooled slightly
1 egg yolk, lightly beaten
½ teaspoon salt
¼ teaspoon garlic powder
1 tablespoon chopped chives
paprika
parsley

Preheat oven to 450°.

In a large bowl, combine mashed potatoes, ¼ cup sour cream, butter, egg yolk, salt and garlic powder. Mixture should be stiff, but pipeable. If too stiff, add a little more sour cream. Place mixture in a large pastry bag fitted with a large rosette tip.

Onto an ungreased baking sheet, pipe mounds about 2½ inches in diameter and about 1½ inches tall to resemble chocolate kisses. Sprinkle with paprika.

Place in middle of oven and bake for 10 to 12 minutes or until edges are set and lightly browned.

Transfer to a serving dish. Garnish with parsley.

Yield: 6 servings (12 kisses)

Alpine Potato Bake

This dish may be assembled ahead and refrigerated until 30 minutes before baking. Sprinkle crumbs on top just before baking.

2	pounds red potatoes, scrubbed
1	cup chopped onion
¼	cup butter
2	tablespoons all-purpose flour
¼	teaspoon pepper
2	cups chicken broth
2	tablespoons spicy brown mustard
1	teaspoon prepared horseradish
¼	cup fine dry bread crumbs

Butter a 2-quart oblong baking dish. In a 3-quart saucepan, cook potatoes in boiling salted water until tender. Drain and let cool.

Preheat oven to 375°. In the same saucepan over medium heat, sauté onion in butter for 10 minutes or until tender and golden. Stir in flour and pepper, then broth. Stirring, bring to a boil and boil for 1 minute. Remove from heat. Whisk in spicy brown mustard and horseradish.

Slice potatoes ½-inch thick. Layer in baking dish. Cover potatoes with sauce and sprinkle with bread crumbs. Bake for 15 to 20 minutes or until hot and bubbly.

Yield: 6 to 8 servings

Tony's Potato Wedges

The crispy coating makes these potatoes special.

> 3   medium baking potatoes, scrubbed (about 1 lb.)
> ¾   cup herb-seasoned stuffing mix, finely crushed
> 2   tablespoons dry spaghetti sauce mix (half of 1½ oz. pkg.)
> ⅓   cup butter or margarine, melted
>   paprika (optional)

Preheat oven to 425°. Coat a 15½ x 10½ x 1-inch jelly roll pan with non-stick spray.

Cut each potato lengthwise into eight equal wedges; set aside.

In a shallow dish or pie plate, mix stuffing mix and spaghetti sauce mix. Dip each potato wedge into melted butter, then coat with crumb mixture. Place wedges on jelly roll pan. Pour remaining butter around wedges.

Bake for 30 to 40 minutes or until fork-tender and golden brown. Sprinkle with paprika if desired.

Yield: 4 servings

Taco Potato Wedges: Substitute 2 tablespoons dry taco seasoning mix for the dry spaghetti sauce mix.

Doctor up a plain baked potato with one of these low-fat, low-calorie toppings: vegetable purées, prepared horseradish, country-style mustard, low-cal salad dressing, or a mixture of chopped tomatoes, green chiles and onions.

Hobo Potatoes

Cook these on the grill and when almost done, start grilling your steaks or hamburgers.

4	medium russet potatoes, cut in ⅜-inch slices (1½ lbs.)
1	cup coarsely chopped onion
1	teaspoon salt
½	teaspoon crushed dried herbs of your choice (Italian seasoning, rosemary or dill)
⅛	teaspoon garlic powder
⅛	teaspoon pepper
2	tablespoons butter or margarine, cut in pieces

Tear off two 18-inch pieces of heavy duty foil. Place potatoes and onion in center of double thickness of foil. Sprinkle potatoes with salt, herbs, garlic powder and pepper; toss lightly. Dot with butter.

Bring two long sides of foil together over potatoes; fold edges over several times to seal, allowing space for steam. Fold short ends up and pinch together to seal securely.

Place packet on grill about 4 inches above medium-hot coals. Turning over several times, cook for 45 to 60 minutes or until potatoes are tender.

Yield: 4 servings

Quick Oven Fries

Try this for a quick snack.

2	large boiling potatoes (about 1 lb.)
2	tablespoons butter or margarine
1	teaspoon dried sage leaves, crushed
⅛	teaspoon pepper
2 to 3	tablespoons grated Parmesan cheese
	dash of onion salt, optional

Preheat oven to 450°. Coat a baking sheet with non-stick vegetable spray; set aside.

Peel potatoes if desired. Cut into ¼-inch slices, then cut each into ¼-inch strips. Place in a medium bowl or pie plate.

In a small saucepan, melt butter. Stir in sage and pepper. Pour over potatoes, tossing until coated. Spread in a single layer on baking sheet.

Bake for 18 to 20 minutes or until browned and tender, stirring occasionally for even browning. Sprinkle Parmesan cheese and, if desired, onion salt over potatoes. Bake 1 minute longer or until cheese is bubbly. Drain on paper towels if desired. Serve immediately.

Yield: 3 to 4 servings

Bistro-Style Potatoes

Serve this hearty potato dish with beer or red wine.

      4   slices bacon, cut in 1-inch pieces
      1   medium onion, halved and sliced
      1   large bay leaf, broken in half
      ½   teaspoon dried thyme leaves, crushed
      ½   teaspoon salt
      ⅛   teaspoon pepper
      4   medium russet potatoes, sliced ⅛-inch thick (1½ lbs.)
      ¼   cup hot water
      1   teaspoon chicken bouillon granules
           chopped parsley, as garnish

Preheat oven to 350°.

In a large skillet over medium heat, sauté bacon until almost done. Remove bacon and set aside. Drain off and reserve bacon drippings. Return skillet to heat.

Add onion, 1 tablespoon of the bacon drippings, bay leaf, thyme, salt and pepper. Sauté onion until limp. Remove onion and bay leaf; set aside.

Sauté potatoes in 1 tablespoon of the bacon drippings, adding more if needed, for 5 minutes or until potatoes begin to brown on edges. Stir in bacon and onion. Transfer to a shallow 1½-quart baking dish or 9-inch pie plate.

In a small bowl, combine water and bouillon granules. Pour evenly over potato mixture.

Bake for 30 to 35 minutes or until potatoes are tender and top is golden. Sprinkle with parsley.

Yield: 3 to 4 servings

No-Curdle Scalloped Potatoes

Baking the potatoes dry before adding the milk keeps them from curdling.

5	russet potatoes (about 1¾ lbs.)
3	tablespoons all-purpose flour
	salt and freshly ground pepper, to taste
3½	tablespoons butter
2	tablespoons finely chopped onion, optional
2	cups hot milk

Preheat oven to 350°. Grease a shallow 1½-quart baking dish.

Peel and thinly slice potatoes (you will need about 6 cups). Place half the potatoes in baking dish. Sprinkle with 1½ tablespoons of the flour and sprinkle with salt and pepper. Dot with 1½ table-spoons butter. If onion is used, place on top of butter. Repeat with remaining potatoes, flour, salt, pepper and butter. Bake for 15 minutes.

Remove from oven. Add hot milk and carefully stir. Bake 1 hour longer or until potatoes are tender.

Yield: 4 servings

Potatoes Anna

A classic potato recipe. Select a pie tin with a dark or dull finish for better browning.

¼	cup butter, melted
4	cups peeled, thinly sliced russet potatoes (4 medium)
½	teaspoon salt or garlic salt
⅛	teaspoon pepper

Preheat oven to 425°. Coat a 9-inch non-stick pie tin with non-stick vegetable spray. Spread bottom and inside of pie tin with about 1½ tablespoons of the melted butter; set aside.

Place potato slices in a towel-lined bowl and gently squeeze to remove excess moisture from potatoes. Remove towel. Toss potatoes with salt and pepper. Arrange one-third of the potato slices in pie tin, starting at center with an overlapping design and packing tightly.

Drizzle with about 1 tablespoon of the butter. Repeat with another third of the potatoes and 1 tablespoon butter, pressing tightly to remove excess air. Top with remaining potatoes and butter. Loosely cover with foil.

Bake for 45 minutes. Uncover. Bake 15 to 20 minutes longer or until fork-tender and golden brown. Carefully tilt pie tin and drain off excess butter. Cut around edge with a knife. Invert potatoes onto an ovenproof serving plate. If desired, broil 6 inches from heat source until browned, protecting rim of plate with strips of foil. Cut in wedges to serve.

Yield: 6 servings

Terrific Tater Skins

Arrange these flavorful snacks on a paper napkin-lined plate or in a basket. They'll disappear quickly!

> 4   medium russet potatoes (about 1½ lbs.)
> flavor variation of choice (see below)

Bake potatoes until tender (see page 9). Cool slightly. Cut in half lengthwise, then cut each half into thirds crosswise, to form six sections from each potato. Scoop pulp from skins, leaving a ¼-inch shell; reserve pulp for another use.

Line a baking sheet with aluminum foil. Prepare flavor variation of your choice. Place potato pieces, skin-side down, on baking sheet. Top as desired. Bake in a 400° oven for 20 to 25 minutes or until skins are crispy and lightly browned. Serve immediately.

Yield: 4 to 6 servings

Cajun Tater Skins: In a small bowl, stir ½ cup melted butter or margarine, 1 teaspoon pepper and ⅛ teaspoon hot pepper sauce. Dip each piece of potato into butter mixture to coat, place on baking sheet and drizzle any remaining butter over the potatoes. Just before serving, sprinkle with paprika and, if desired, salt.

Herbed Tater Skins: In a small bowl, stir ½ cup melted butter or margarine, 1¼ teaspoons each crushed dried dill weed and onion salt, ¼ teaspoon garlic powder and a dash of pepper. Dip each piece of potato into butter mixture to coat, place on baking sheet and drizzle any remaining butter over the potatoes. Garnish with sour cream before serving.

Nacho Tater Skins: In a small bowl, stir 1 cup each shredded Monterey Jack and Colby cheese and ½ teaspoon chili powder. Generously sprinkle over potato skins. After baking, top with your choice of sliced jalapeño peppers, sliced olives, chopped pimento or diced green chiles.

BAKED
GOODS

Jiffy Yeast Rolls

You can have fresh-baked yeast rolls ready in less than two hours.

¾ cup unseasoned mashed potatoes
¾ cup water
2 tablespoons butter or margarine
2¼ cups all-purpose flour
2 tablespoons sugar
1 package active dry yeast
1 teaspoon salt
1 large egg
1 tablespoon sesame or poppy seeds, optional

In a small saucepan over low heat, combine the mashed potatoes, water and butter. Stir until very warm (120° to 130°, butter may not be completely melted).

Meanwhile, in a 1-quart bowl, whisk together flour, sugar, yeast and salt. Gradually stir in warm potato mixture and egg until blended. Beat vigorously for 2 minutes. Cover and let rise in a warm place, free from drafts, for 30 minutes or until doubled.

Spoon into well-greased muffin cups, about ¼ cup batter in each. (The mixture will be elastic.) If desired, sprinkle with sesame or poppy seeds. Let rise for 15 minutes, uncovered, in a warm place that is free from drafts.

Bake in a preheated 400° oven for 15 to 17 minutes or until golden brown. Serve hot.

Yield: 12 rolls

Old-Fashioned Chocolate Cake

Potato is the secret ingredient in this very moist cake.

2	cups all-purpose flour
2	cups sugar
1	cup unseasoned mashed potatoes, room temperature
¾	cup milk
4	ounces semisweet chocolate, melted and cooled
3	eggs
⅓	cup butter or margarine, softened
1 ¼	teaspoons baking soda
1	teaspoon salt
1	teaspoon vanilla extract
½	teaspoon baking powder
	Chocolate Frosting (see below)
	chopped pecans or walnuts, as garnish

Preheat oven to 350°. Grease and lightly flour a 13 x 9 x 2-inch baking pan. In a large mixer bowl at low speed, beat flour, sugar, mashed potatoes, milk, chocolate, eggs, butter, baking soda, salt, vanilla and baking powder for 30 seconds, scraping sides frequently. Increase speed to high and beat for 3 minutes, scraping bowl occasionally. Pour into pan.

Bake for 40 to 45 minutes or until top springs back when lightly pressed and a wooden toothpick inserted in center comes out clean. Place pan on a wire rack and cool completely. Top with Chocolate Frosting and decorate with chopped nuts, if desired.

Yield: 12 to 15 servings

Chocolate Frosting

In a small mixer bowl at medium speed, beat ⅓ cup softened butter with 3 ounces melted unsweetened chocolate until smooth. At low speed, beat in 3½ cups powdered sugar. Beat in 4 tablespoons milk, 1 teaspoon vanilla extract and a dash of salt. Beat until smooth, adding additional milk if needed. **Yield:** 2 cups.

Vegetarian Cake

This moist cake is a delicious, healthy twist on fruitcake. Serve it "as is" or drizzle with Vanilla Glaze and decorate the top with red and green candied cherries.

2	cups all-purpose flour
3	teaspoons baking powder
1½	teaspoons ground cinnamon
1½	teaspoons ground allspice
¾	teaspoon baking soda
¼	teaspoon salt
1½	cups peeled, shredded apples (2 medium)
1½	cups peeled, shredded carrots (3 medium)
1½	cups peeled, shredded potatoes (about 2 medium)
¾	cup currants
¾	cup raisins
¾	cup chopped walnuts
1	tablespoon grated orange peel
1½	cups packed brown sugar
¾	cup butter or margarine, softened
3	eggs
2	tablespoons light molasses

Preheat oven to 350°. Generously grease and flour a 10-inch fluted tube pan.

Onto waxed paper sift the flour, baking powder, cinnamon, allspice, baking soda and salt; set aside.

In a medium bowl, stir apples, carrots, potatoes, currants, raisins, nuts and orange peel; set aside.

In a large mixer bowl at medium speed, beat brown sugar and butter until fluffy. Add eggs and molasses and beat until well blended. At low speed, beat in dry ingredients until moistened. Gradually add vegetable mixture and beat until well blended. Spoon into pan. Bake for 60 minutes or until a wooden pick inserted 1 inch from outer edge comes out clean and cake pulls away from pan. Cool on a wire rack for 10 minutes; remove cake from pan and cool completely.

Cover and store in the refrigerator. This cake is best served the second day. Slice with a sharp knife.

Vanilla Glaze

This all-purpose glaze has many uses. Try it on Vegetarian Cake, or as an icing for doughnuts, cinnamon rolls or baked goods.

2	cups sifted powdered sugar
¼	cup half-and-half
1	tablespoon butter, softened
½	teaspoon vanilla extract

In a small mixer bowl at medium speed, beat powered sugar, half- and-half, butter and vanilla until smooth and creamy.

Yield: ¾ cup

Apricot Scones

These scones can be made ahead as they freeze and reheat well.

½	cup snipped dried apricots
	hot tap water
1½	cups all-purpose flour
¼	cup sugar
1½	teaspoons baking powder
½	teaspoon salt
⅛	teaspoon ground cinnamon
⅓	cup butter or margarine, chilled
¾	cup unseasoned mashed potatoes
1	egg
3	tablespoons milk
1	tablespoon sliced almonds
1	teaspoon sugar

Preheat oven to 400°. Lightly grease a baking sheet.

Cover apricots with water and let stand for 10 minutes.

Meanwhile, in a large bowl, combine flour, ¼ cup sugar, baking powder, salt and cinnamon. With a pastry blender or two knives, cut in butter until mixture resembles coarse crumbs. Thoroughly drain apricots. Stir apricots and mashed potatoes into flour mixture.

In a small bowl, whisk together egg and milk; set ½ tablespoon of the mixture aside. Stir remaining mixture into flour mixture just until dry ingredients are moistened. Knead 6 to 8 times to form a ball. Place on baking sheet. Flatten into a 7-inch circle. With a floured knife, cut into six wedges, but do not separate.

Brush top with reserved egg-milk mixture. Sprinkle with almonds and 1 teaspoon sugar.

Bake for 22 to 24 minutes or until lightly browned. Serve immediately with butter and jam or honey.

Yield: 6 servings